Project 7-11

Back to Bas

ENGLISH

for 10-11 year olds

Sheila Lane and Marion Kemp

The alphabet

▸ Write the complete alphabet.

| A | | | | | | | | | | | | | | | | | | | | | | | | | Z |

▸ Write the missing letters in each series.

1 A B ☐ D E ☐ G H ☐ J K
2 ☐ P Q ☐ S T ☐ V W
3 Z Y X ☐ V U T ☐ R Q P ☐
4 C ☐ E ☐ ☐ H ☐ J ☐ ☐ M ☐ O ☐ ☐
5 S ☐ ☐ P ☐ N ☐ ☐ K ☐ I ☐ ☐

Fiction books in a library are arranged in alphabetical order of the authors' surnames.

▸ Write these authors' names in **alphabetical order**.

Alison Uttley   _____
Nina Bawden   _____
Philippa Pearce   _____
Eric Williams   _____
Arthur Ransome   _____

When words in a set begin with the **same** letter, look at the **second** letter of the word. When they begin with the **same two letters**, look at the **third** letter and so on...

▸ Write these authors' names in **alphabetical order**.

Alcott _____   Berg _____   Garfield _____
Aesop _____   Bennett _____   Gard _____
Andersen _____   Bell _____   Garvey _____
Adams _____   Beckett _____   Garland _____
Appiah _____   Betts _____   Garner _____

CHALLENGE

Crack the code!
Find the title of a book written in alphabet code.

P M J W F S   U X J T U

_____ _____

The dictionary

Words beginning with A to D are found, roughly, in the first part.
Words beginning with E to L are found, roughly, in the second part.
Words beginning with M to R are found, roughly, in the third part.
Words beginning with S to Z are found, roughly, in the fourth part.

Read the words in the box.

Write the words from the box in the correct dictionary part.

cask   sole
lush   gulf
septic   rouse
fawn   blend
phobia   vice
appal   kebab
tamper   pride
mural   bluff

1st part

2nd part

3rd part

4th part

Write true or false for each statement.

astronomer: a person who studies birds _____ ☐

interview: a break or gap _____ ☐

microscope: an instrument for magnifying tiny things _____ ☐

tentacle: part of a shelter made of canvas _____ ☐

zoology: the scientific study of animals _____ ☐

Check your answers by using your dictionary.

Use your dictionary to help you to write **clues** for this word puzzle.

1	m	a	s	s	i	v	e		
2	m	e	d	i	e	v	a	l	
3	m	i	n	i	a	t	u	r	e
4	m	o	d	e	r	n			
5	m	o	n	o	t	o	n	o	u	s

1 _____
2 _____
3 _____
4 _____
5 _____

3

Grammar

	Parts of speech			
A **noun** is a **naming** word.	An **adjective** describes a noun.	A **pronoun** stands for a noun.	A **verb** tells what is being done.	

Colour in the **one** word in each row which tells you the name of the **part of speech** which the other words belong to. Fill in the empty space with another example of that part of speech.

1	coat	noun	cloak	jacket	anorak
2	dirty		dusty	adjective	tarnished
3	him	her		us	pronoun
4		bounded	sprang	verb	plunged
5	dejected		adjective	gloomy	miserable
6	robbed	burgled	verb		stole

Write **nouns** of your own choice, in the spaces.

1 The postman brought two _____ and a _____.

2 I enjoy reading _____ and _____.

3 We celebrate _____ in the month of _____.

4 _____ and _____ are capital cities.

Write a suitable **verb** in each sentence.

1 I _____ my new bicycle as far as the park.

2 The artist was _____ a picture of the lake.

3 Wild geese _____ over the tops of the trees.

4 A cook can _____ food in an oven.

Draw rings round the **nouns** and write the missing **pronouns**.

1 When Tom tried to skate _____ fell flat on _____ face.

2 The children promised that _____ would return early.

3 Jane and John said, "_____ will go now."

4 When my mother lost _____ purse _____ was upset.

4

Missing words

The clue to the missing word in each of these sentences is in the **meaning** of the sentence itself.

✏️ Draw a ring round the word in each box which makes the best sense in each sentence.

| bright   cheerful   old |

There was a strange, creepy feeling in the _____ manor house that night.

| dogs   owls   cats |

Doors banged, windows flew open and _____ hooted in the tall trees.

| velvety   soft   metal |

Suddenly, on the winding staircase, there was the clank of _____ chains.

Read **all** the paragraph.

✏️ Write the most suitable adjective from the **suggestions box** in the right space.

The dreadful ghost stood quite still in the __pale__ moonlight. He was an __2__ man of __3__ appearance. His eyes were as red as __4__ coals. __5__ grey hair fell over his __6__ shoulders. From his __7__ wrists hung __8__ chains.

Suggestions box

1. warm   pale   sunny
2. old   young   pleasant
3. gentle   terrible   thick
4. burning   dead   black
5. Short   Long   Woollen
6. handsome   hunched   elegant
7. brave   bony   brainy
8. prickly   slimy   rusty

✏️ Rewrite the paragraph with adjectives of your own choice to make another frightening picture of **a ghost**.

_____
_____
_____
_____
_____
_____
_____

Sentences

A **sentence** is a group of words which is complete in itself.
Every sentence has a verb.
A sentence begins with a capital letter and ends with a full stop,
a question mark or an exclamation mark.

Examples: Please remember to bring your book back.
           Have you remembered your book?
           You have forgotten your book again!

Show which of the following are complete **sentences** by putting a ✓ or a ✗.

1 I gave my books to the librarian.
2 *Treasure Island* and *Kidnapped*
3 In the reference section
4 I'll return all my books next week.
5 My favourite author

Complete these groups of words to make complete **sentences** with correct punctuation.

1 Tomorrow's match _____
2 Where will you _____
3 What a foolish _____
4 _____ due back on Friday.
5 Can you tell me _____

Divide **each** of these paragraphs into four **sentences** with correct punctuation and capital letters.

1 one of my hobbies is cooking for a Victoria sponge I use self-raising flour soft margarine caster sugar and eggs although butter has an excellent flavour you can make a very good cake with margarine eggs should be at room temperature and not used straight from the refrigerator

2 Land's End is the south-west tip of the British mainland each year over a million people visit the area just over a mile offshore is the Longships reef this danger to ships is guarded by the Longships lighthouse

A sentence has two parts, a **subject** and a **predicate**.
The **subject** tells **who** or **what** the sentence is about.
The **predicate** tells what is **said** about the **subject**.

e.g. | **Sentence** | **Subject** | **Predicate** |
| --- | --- | --- |
| Fish swim in the sea. | Fish | swim in the sea. |
| A savage dog barked. | A savage dog | barked. |

 Underline the **subject** and draw brackets round the **predicate** in each of the following sentences.

1 The <u>thief</u> (jumped over the wall).
2 A policeman ran after him.
3 The angry shopkeeper waved his fist.
4 A crowd soon gathered near the scene.

1 Two silly sheep wandered away from the flock.
2 The old shepherd gave a short whistle.
3 His sheep dog crept quietly round the wanderers.
4 The flock was soon together again.

The **subject** of a sentence must **agree** with its **verb**.
A **singular subject** has a **singular verb**.
A **plural subject** has a **plural verb**.

e.g. Jane <u>plays</u> the piano.   The <u>star is</u> shining.

   The <u>girls play</u> the piano.   The <u>stars are</u> shining.

 Underline the **subject** and draw a ring round the correct **verb** in each of the following sentences.

1 <u>You</u> (is (are)) very early today.
2 Some children (has have) to be in bed by seven o'clock.
3 We (was were) too late for the match.
4 They (go goes) on holiday tomorrow.
5 I will (meet meets) you at two o'clock.
6 James (do does) his best to keep up with the others.

7

Synonyms

> A **synonym** is a word having the **same meaning**, or nearly the same meaning, as another word.
> e.g. big: colossal   enormous   gigantic   huge

Read the words in the box.

 Arrange the words in the box as **pairs of synonyms**.

```
bright✓  pitiful   beg
crowd    lively   locality
district vivid✓   pathetic
active   plead    inactive
multitude  idle
```

__bright__ and __vivid__
_____ and _____
_____ and _____
_____ and _____
_____ and _____
_____ and _____
_____ and _____

 Draw a ring round the word in each line which is a **synonym** of the word in capital letters.

ABANDON   gather   plentiful   (leave)
ABSURD   deep   ridiculous   bad
ATTEMPT   attack   fasten   try
EXTERIOR   amount   outside   inside
IMITATE   mimic   delay   invent
MARGIN   raid   edge   centre
MANUFACTURE   write   instruct   make
SURRENDER   yield   surround   fight
DIMINUTIVE   round   quiet   small
TRANSPARENT   clear   transport   opaque

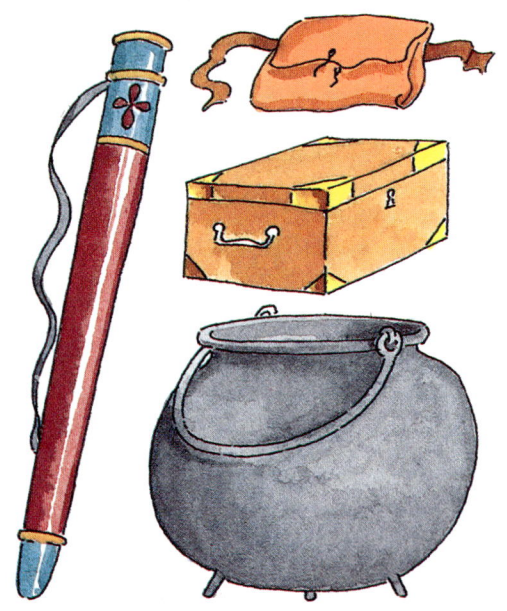

CHALLENGE

Write the name of something you could expect to find in each of these containers.

a goblet _____   a casket _____   a cauldron _____

a pouch _____   a cistern _____   a decanter _____

a wardrobe _____   a butt _____   a scabbard _____

The Thesaurus

A **Thesaurus** collects together words which have a **similar meaning** to each other.
e.g. glad, joyful, cheerful all mean happy

> Write **synonyms** for these **key words**.
> Use your dictionary to help you.

Key word: **little** (adjective)
Synonyms: 1 _tiny_
2 _____
3 _____

Key word: **bright** (adjective)
Synonyms: 1 _____
2 _____
3 _____

Key word: a **book** (noun)
Synonyms: 1 _____
2 _____
3 _____

Key word: a **box** (noun)
Synonyms: 1 _____
2 _____
3 _____

Key word: to **cut** (verb)
Synonyms: 1 _____
2 _____
3 _____

Key word: to **kill** (verb)
Synonyms: 1 _____
2 _____
3 _____

A **Thesaurus** can help you to choose the best word for your purpose.

> Write the best word from the brackets to describe:

a brave soldier (courageous, trusty, strong) _courageous_
horrible weather (smelly, damp, ghastly) _____
an ugly building (forbidding, haunted, hideous) _____
a tasty meal (charming, intelligent, delicious) _____
dirty shoes (soiled, untidy, wet) _____
the pretty dress (tidy, smart, beautiful) _____
an old person (antique, aged, historical) _____
rich people (fruity, expensive, wealthy) _____
the weak patient (feeble, broken, thin) _____
a pleasant smell (strong, fragrant, picturesque) _____

Comprehension

✏️ Write [yes] or [no] or [don't know] after each question.

1 Is geography the study of people who lived in the past? _____
2 Is a book of maps called an atlas? _____
3 Is the Dead Sea in England? _____
4 Is there such a place as Kicking Horse Pass? _____

Read this true information:

> Geography is the study of the Earth's surface; its lands, seas, oceans; its climate; its people, where they live and what they produce.
>
> Geographical information is found in a book of maps, called an atlas. The word 'atlas' comes from the name of a Greek giant, who is said to have carried the heavens on his shoulders.
>
> The giant Atlas also gave his name to a range of mountains in North Africa. In an atlas there are many unusual place names such as: Table Mountain in South Africa; Kicking Horse Pass in Canada; the River Darling in Australia; the Dead Sea in Israel and Lake Titicaca in South America.

✏️ Mark your [yes] and [no] answers with a [✓] or [X].

✏️ Answer these questions in sentences.

1 What do you find in an atlas?
_____

2 What do people who study geography learn about?
_____

3 Where does the word 'atlas' come from?
_____

✏️ Write the meaning of: Use your dictionary to help you.

island _____
lake _____
climate _____
population _____

Making notes

Read each sentence.

 Cross out the words **not** important to the meaning.

 Write the four **key words** in each sentence as...

Sentence **Notes**

1 A̶n̶ ocean i̶s̶ a̶ large area o̶f̶ sea.   ocean, large, area, sea
2 A continent is a large mass of land.
3 Asia is the world's largest continent.
4 Greenland is the largest island in the world.
5 The longest river in the world is the Nile.

 Write the **key words** in each sentence as **notes**.

1 A lake is an area of water surrounded by land.
2 A tributary is a river which flows into another river.
3 A river is a stream of water flowing into another river, sea or lake.
4 A ford is a shallow place where people can wade or drive across a river.

1 _____
2 _____
3 _____
4 _____

Read this paragraph:

A waterfall is a flow of water over cliffs or rocks. The Victoria Falls, named after Queen Victoria, are in Zambia. Another famous waterfall is in the United States where water from the Niagara river pours over the Niagara Falls.

 Write **notes** for each of the three sentences.

1 _____
2 _____
3 _____

Spelling

 Use colours to identify the letter string in each word in the box.

entr(ance)	suspicious	thought	slaughter
ought	bought	daughter	substance
caught ✓	performance	balance	delicious
taught	precious	brought	previous

 Fill in the word chains with words from the box.

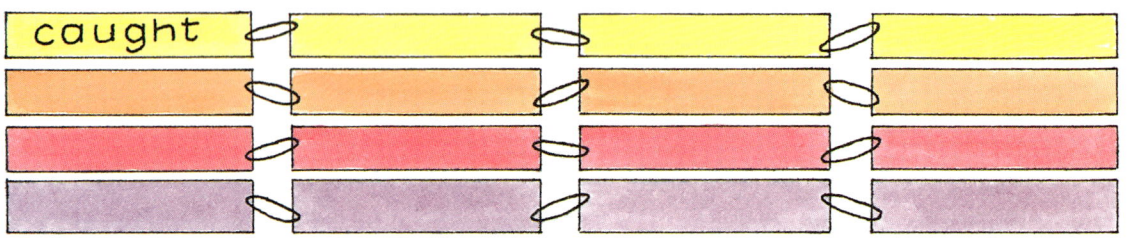

Use words from the box to complete these sentences.

1 After the cruel hunters had _____ the young seals, they began to _____ them with heavy clubs.

2 The _____ policeman frowned and asked the motorist if he had any _____ convictions.

3 We hurried in through the _____ to the theatre just as the _____ was beginning.

4 The hardworking boy _____ that he _____ to complete his work.

CHALLENGE

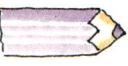 Take letters from the **end** of the first word and the **beginning** of the second word to make the names of living creatures.

enor(mous e)nvelope   damp igloo

plastic rabbit   correct route

white elephant   frantic rower

Punctuation

> ___,___ A comma written above the line is an **apostrophe**.
> One use of an apostrophe is to show where letters have been missed out in the **short forms** of words
>   e.g. do<u>n't</u> for do <u>not</u>

 Write these words **in full**.

1 I'm __I am__ 2 what's _____ 3 aren't _____
4 he's _____ 5 hasn't _____ 6 couldn't _____

 Write the **short forms** of these words.

1 I have _____ 2 where is _____ 3 is not _____
4 she is _____ 5 cannot _____ 6 would not _____

Another use of an apostrophe is to show **ownership**.
  e.g. Mary**'s** coat.   The **s** shows that the coat **belongs** to Mary.

 Add an **apostrophe** to the owner's name in each phrase.

1 Father's watch   2 a sailors monkey
3 Mothers chair   4 a horses mane
5 Pauls book   6 Spots tail

When a plural noun ends with an **s**, the apostrophe is written **after** the **s** to show **ownership**.

  e.g. the boy**s'** coats   The **s** shows that there is **more than one** boy owning the coats.

 Add an **apostrophe** to the owners' names in these sentences.

1 Some birds feathers are brightly coloured.
2 The girls shoes were left in the gym.
3 All the dogs names were written on the kennels.
4 Ladies hats can be very attractive.
5 The knives handles were made of ivory.

Main verbs and auxiliary verbs

Some verbs are 'helper' or **auxiliary verbs**.
e.g. Janet <u>is</u> my friend. In this sentence, <u>is</u> stands alone as the **main verb**.

Janet <u>is</u> <u>coming</u> to tea. In this sentence <u>is</u> acts as the **auxiliary verb**.

Write **main verb** or **auxiliary verb** for each underlined verb.

1 I <u>am</u> a boy. _____
2 My parents <u>are</u> coming home. _____
3 I <u>am</u> going home. _____
4 My father <u>is</u> a builder. _____
5 They <u>were</u> late. _____
6 I <u>was</u> laughing happily. _____

Rewrite these sentences, using <u>is</u>, <u>are</u>, <u>was</u> or <u>were</u> as **auxiliary verbs**.

1 We (is, are) going home.

2 They (was, were) running away.

3 I (was, were) going out.

4 She (is, are) playing the flute.

5 She (is, are) swimming.

6 The twins (were, was) playing tennis.

Read the words in the box.

| has | am | been |
| have | be | being |

Use the words from the box as **auxiliary verbs** to complete each sentence.

1 They _____ left the school
2 Is that cat _____ playful?
3 John _____ left his coat.
4 I've _____ reading a book.
5 I _____ going home.
6 Will you _____ coming tomorrow?

CHALLENGE

Fill in the missing letters to make words which are **synonyms** of the word 'helping'.

| a | u | x | | | | | y |

| s | u | p | | | | | g |

| a | d | d | | | | | l |

| s | u | p | | | | | | y |

Tense of verbs

A verb can be in the **past**, or the **present**, or the **future**.
This is called the **tense** of the verb.

Past — Yesterday's date was 24th April.
Present — Today's date is 25th April.
Future — Tomorrow's date will be 26th April.

Write **past tense**, **present tense** or **future tense** at the end of each sentence.

1 Today is my birthday. — *present tense*
2 William Shakespeare was born in the 16th century. _____
3 I shall be going to the Carnival next Saturday. _____
4 Columbus crossed the Atlantic in 1492. _____
5 The train will stop at all stations to London. _____
6 Those aeroplanes are immediately overhead. _____

Write the **past tense** of the verb in capital letters in each sentence.

1 PAINT   Sir Joshua Reynolds __painted__ portraits.
2 CARVE   Grinling Gibbons _____ wooden panels.
3 DESIGN Christopher Wren _____ many famous buildings.
4 INVENT The Kellogg brothers _____ cornflakes.
5 COMPOSE Handel _____ music.
6 DISCOVER Marie Curie _____ radium.

1 WRITE   William Shakespeare __wrote__ Macbeth.
2 FIGHT   Nelson _____ the Battle of Trafalgar.
3 COME   William the Conqueror _____ to England from Normandy.
4 SEE   King Alfred _____ the cakes burning.
5 FLY   Amy Johnson _____ from England to Australia.
6 BRING   Sir Walter Raleigh _____ tobacco to Elizabethan England.

Antonyms

An **antonym** is a word having an **opposite** meaning to another word.
e.g. big – small   ugly – beautiful

Read the words in the box.

often ✓	detect
fresh	seldom ✓
ascend	conceal
rancid	descend

Arrange the words in the box as pairs of **antonyms**.

often ... _seldom_
_____ ... _____
_____ ... _____
_____ ... _____

Draw a ring round the word in each line which is an **antonym** of the word in capital letters.

1 FEW   three   (many)   amount   calculate
2 TERMINATE   stop   holiday   end   begin
3 EXPAND   elastic   stretch   contract   explain
4 MAXIMUM   most   minimum   saying   minute
5 NEGLIGENT   thoughtless necessary   careless   attentive

Some **antonyms** are formed by the addition of a group of letters at the beginning of a word e.g. appear – **dis**appear

Write an **antonym** for each of the following using:

dis-   un-   im-   or   il-

possible _____   obedient _____   suitable _____
healthy _____   legible _____   approve _____

Rewrite each sentence, using words you have made, to give the underlined words an **opposite** meaning.

1 Suitable food helps to make people healthy.

_____

2 It is possible to read legible handwriting.

_____

3 Most teachers approve of obedient children.

_____

16

Prefixes and suffixes

A **prefix** is a letter, or a group of letters, at the **beginning** of a word. e.g. 'trans' – meaning across or beyond

Write the meaning of each word. Use your dictionary to help you.

1 transatlantic _____
2 transfer _____
3 transplant _____
4 transport _____

Write a complete word beginning with each of the following **prefixes** and give the meaning of each one. Use your dictionary to help you.

bi-	_bicycle_	_a two-wheeled vehicle_
tri-	_____	_____
cent-	_____	_____
circum-	_____	_____
octo-	_____	_____

A **suffix** is a group of letters at the **end** of a word.
e.g. enjoy**able** peace**ful** poison**ous**

Change each noun into an adjective by adding a **suffix**.

danger _____ break _____ bliss _____ colour _____

Write an **adjective** in each sentence formed from the noun in the brackets.

1 Poisons are _____ substances. (harm)
2 The sick child made a _____ recovery. (remark)
3 It was _____ to try to stop the rush of water. (hope)
4 The _____ fireman entered the burning building. (courage)

Comprehension

Read about The Olympic Games.

1. The Olympic Games originated at Olympia, in Greece, nearly 3,000 years ago. The Festival lasted five days and was in honour of Zeus, the King of the Greek gods. The Games were timed to take place between harvesting grain, which finished in early August and gathering grapes and olives, which began in the middle of September.

 Underline the **one** title which best expresses the **main idea** for the whole paragraph.

a) Farming in Ancient Greece
b) The King of the Gods
c) The Origin of the Olympic Games

2. Athletics took place in the stadium on the second day of the Festival. One of these events was the Pentathlon, which consisted of five events. These were running, wrestling, throwing the discus, throwing the javelin and long jump. Greek long jumpers carried weights in their hands which they threw away on landing.

 Underline the **one** title which best expresses the **main idea** for the whole paragraph.

a) Wrestling
b) Athletic Events on the Second Day of the Festival
c) How to Make a Long Jump

 Answer these questions in sentences.

1 Where did the Olympic Games originate?

___

2 Why did the Games take place between early August and the middle of September?

___

___

3 What did the Pentathlon consist of?

___

___

Read all of each paragraph about the Modern Olympics.

Write the word from the box which best fits the meaning in the spaces.

eg The Marathon race starts and finishes in the [1 **stadium**]. It is run over a [2 **total**] distance of 26 miles 385 yards.

1	church	(stadium)	school
2	width	volume	(total)

1. The starter of a track event gives the [1], 'On your mark ... Set ...!' When all the competitors are [2] he fires the starting [3]. The winner is the [4] to reach the finishing post with any part of his [5] her torso.

1	speech	command	lecture
2	dressed	lucky	still
3	tape	pistol	torpedo
4	second	last	first
5	or	and	but

2. The game of hockey is played with two [1], each having eleven players. Each team is [2] allowed two substitutes in case of [3]. To score a goal the ball must pass [4] the opponent's [5].

1	hands	swarms	teams
2	and	too	also
3	injury	pain	wound
4	between	into	beside
5	bag	bin	net

3. Diving [1] consist of high-board and springboard events. The diver must enter the water with his or [2] body straight, either head [3] feet first. Feet must be [4] and toes must be pointed. Marks for diving [5] given out of ten.

1	compositions	competitions	
	comparisons		
2	she	her	him
3	and	but	or
4	together	anyhow	always
5	is	be	are

Sentences

A **simple** sentence makes a statement or asks a question about **one** thing.
A **simple** sentence contains **one** verb.
  eg Airmen fly in aeroplanes.

Subject (who or what the sentence is about) – Airmen ...
Predicate (what is said about the subject) – fly in aeroplanes.
Verb – fly.

 Divide each sentence into **subject** and **predicate**. Underline the **verb**.

Sentence	Subject	Predicate
1 Doctors examine patients.	Doctors	examine patients.
2 Dentists extract teeth.	_____	_____
3 Soldiers protect their country.	_____	_____
4 A judge presides in court.	_____	_____
5 An optician tests eyesight.	_____	_____

Two simple sentences can be joined together with **and**, **but** or **or** to make a **compound** sentence.

e.g. **Simple sentences**   **A compound sentence**
Airmen fly in aeroplanes.   Airmen fly in aeroplanes, **but**
Sailors sail in ships.   sailors sail in ships.

Join each pair of simple sentences to make **one** compound sentence, using **and**, **but** or **or**.

1 Don't walk on that glass.
  You will cut your feet.

1 _____

2 We looked for the treasure.
  We couldn't find it.

2 _____

3 The car was out of control.
  It crashed into a wall.

3 _____

Complete the following to make **compound** sentences.

1 I slipped on the ice, but _____

2 I had to choose between a book or _____

3 I ran into the garden and _____

Joining words

> A word which **joins** two sentences or two groups of words is called a **joining word**. Some common **joining words** are:
> and   or   but   as   so   if   before   after   because
> although   until   unless   since   while

   Draw a ring round the **joining words** in each sentence.

1 I went to school although I felt unwell.
2 I shall be early if I hurry.
3 You will be late unless you go now.
4 I was on time because I walked quickly.
5 I waited outside until the staff arrived.

   Complete these sentences with a **joining word**.

1 Would you prefer an orange _____ an apple?
2 John closed his eyes _____ went to sleep.
3 I lost my purse _____ I went to the police station.
4 I intended to swim in the sea _____ the water was cold.
5 We hurried to the shops _____ they closed.

   Write suitable **joining words** in the spaces in this paragraph.

The old sow fed her babies _____ they began to fall asleep. She was hoping for a rest, _____ she was soon disappointed. One young piglet began to squeal _____ he was still hungry. Another would have suffocated _____ his mother hadn't turned him over with her snout. Then, to the mother's dismay, they all woke up _____ clamoured for more milk.

CHALLENGE

x	i	o	r	z	b	u	t
a	f	t	e	r	e	x	y
s	y	s	i	n	c	e	z
z	x	o	y	z	a	x	y
a	l	t	h	o	u	g	h
n	x	y	z	y	s	x	z
d	z	u	n	l	e	s	s

Can you find nine **joining words**?

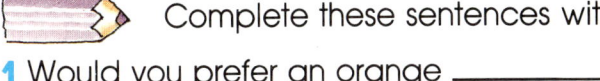   Ring each one, then write them here:

_____
_____
_____
_____
_____

Grammar

> An **adverb** tells more **about a verb**.
>
> e.g. Anna answered <u>correctly</u>.   The adverb <u>correctly</u> tells **how** Anna answered.

 Draw a line under the **verb** and a ring around the **adverb** in each sentence.

1. I <u>whispered</u> (softly).
2. He spoke loudly.
3. We ate hungrily.
4. The child wept bitterly.
5. They danced gracefully.
6. She listened carefully.

> Many adverbs end in **-ly**.   e.g. quick**ly** hopeful**ly**

 Complete each sentence with an **adverb** formed from the adjective in capital letters.

1. SOFT   The snow fell ___softly___ from the trees.
2. RAPID   A fire spread _____ to the second floor.
3. CLEAR   The teacher explained the problem _____.
4. AWKWARD   My painful foot made me walk _____.
5. POLITE   John raised his cap _____ to the old lady.
6. DISTINCT   From the cliffs we could see the ship _____.

> Adverbs tell **how**, **when** or **where** the action of the verb takes place.
>
> e.g. The dog <u>ran</u> (away).   Away tells **where** the dog ran.
>
>   The dog (always) barked.   Always tells **when** the dog barked.
>
>   The dog <u>ate</u> (hungrily).   Hungrily tells **how** the dog ate.

 Draw a line under the **verb** and a ring around the **adverb** in each sentence.

1. I (sometimes) <u>make</u> the toast.
2. I went away for the weekend.
3. A train will arrive shortly.
4. I walked sideways down the corridor.
5. My mother always cooks my supper.
6. The door opened immediately.

English usage

> To make **comparisons** of adverbs ending with **-ly**, add **more** or **most**.
> e.g. quickly – **more** quickly   **most** quickly

Write the **missing forms** for these adverbs.

1 QUIETLY — *more quietly* — *most quietly*
2 GRACIOUSLY
3 DEEPLY
4 SERIOUSLY
5 DESPERATELY
6 HAPPILY

> For some adverbs **new** words are formed to make comparisons.
> e.g. bad   worse   worst

Underline the correct **form** in each of the following.

1 I was not well yesterday, but today I feel (weller, <u>better</u>).
2 My results were good, but my sister's were (better, gooder).
3 Of the three instruments, I like the piano (bestest, best).
4 Jo did badly in the test, but Janet did (more bad, worse) and Mary did (worser, worst) of all.

Write the meaning of each adverb.

Use each one in a sentence of your own.

1 seldom
2 never
3 frequently
4 occasionally
5 always

Spelling

Say these words aloud. Draw a ring round the silent letter in each one.

(w)hole   combed   answer   guess   knowledge   psalm

ghost   reign   autumn   wrinkle   plumber   knot

> Letter 'c' can make a 'hard' sound as in (c)orrect, or a 'soft' sound as in (c)entre.
> Letter 'g' can make a 'hard' sound as in re(g)ular, or a 'soft' sound as in (g)enius.

Say each word aloud. Draw a ring round the letters in those words having a **'hard c'** sound or a **'hard g'** sound.

city   cruel   centimetre   gentle   guitar   imagine

(c)ough   ceiling   educate   (g)uide   geometry   ungrateful

discolour   curious   uncertain   beginning   ghastly   ginger

Write the words having a **'soft c'** sound.

Write the words having a **'soft g'** sound.

_____ _____

_____ _____

LOOK at each word.   **SAY** each word.   **COVER** each word.   **WRITE** from memory.   **CHECK** your spelling.

| circle |
| calendar |
| graph |
| signature |
| guitar |
| palace |
| ghost |
| cylinder |

CHALLENGE

What have **all** these words got in common?   Read them aloud and L I S [T] E N !

thistle   ballet   castle   soften

glisten   chalet   hustle   christen

Punctuation revision

▸ Write the correct **punctuation mark** in each box.

| full stop | comma | question mark | exclamation mark | inverted commas | apostrophe |

▸ Write the correct **punctuation marks** in each balloon.

1 I saw two fire engines ◯ an ambulance and a police car at the scene ◯
2 A policeman shouted ◯ ◯ Stand back ◯ ◯ to all the onlookers ◯
3 ◯ ◯ What is your name ◯ ◯ asked a newspaper reporter ◯
4 ◯ ◯ Write your address on this note-pad ◯ ◯ he continued ◯ and I will send you a copy of *The Echo* ◯ ◯
5 In spite of feeling nervous ◯ I plucked up courage and said ◯ ◯ Will I see my name in print ◯ ◯

▸ Write the short forms of the following, using **apostrophes**.

I am here.   __I'm here.__   I cannot come. _____
It is cold. _____   Do not go yet. _____
Who is there? _____   She is absent. _____
That is right. _____   Where is my hat? _____

▸ Add **apostrophes** to the names of the owners in the following.

1 the Queens son   2 all the childrens books
3 the babys mother   4 Andrews coat
5 a firemans helmet   6 the three giants footmarks
7 ladies handbags   8 Ahmets brother

> A full stop is used to show that letters have been left off the end of a word in an **abbreviation**. e.g. **B.C.** – **B**efore **C**hrist

CHALLENGE

Find the meaning of:

P.T.O.   P.S.   U.K.   R.I.P.
C.O.D.   M.A.   U.S.A. R.S.V.P.

Comprehension

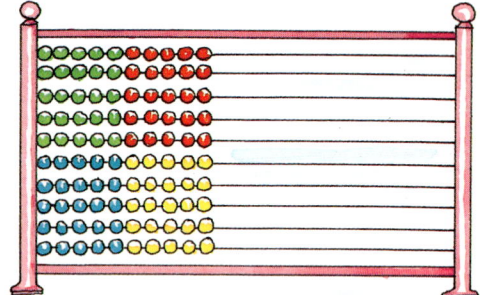

Read about The First Computers.

1 The Abacus, invented in China more than 2,000 years ago, was a simple calculating frame. Shallow grooves were made in a tablet of clay so that small stones could be used for addition and subtraction. Later, the stones, which could easily be lost, were replaced by beads threaded on wire. The word 'calculator' comes from the Latin word **calculus**, meaning 'little stone'.

 Underline the **one** title which best expresses the **main idea** for the whole paragraph.

a) All About Stones
b) The Development of the Abacus
c) Life in Ancient China

2 In 1833 the first real computer was designed by an Englishman named Charles Babbage. Calculations in Babbage's machine were made from a series of punched cards which worked automatically. This machine, which could store information, was the first digital calculator. The word 'digital' comes from the Latin word **digitus**, meaning 'finger, toe'.

 Underline the **one** title which best expresses the **main idea** for the whole paragraph.

a) How to Punch Cards
b) Storing Information
c) The First Computer

Fill in **details** about The First Computers.

1 The Abacus originated in _____.
2 The Latin word _____ means 'little stone'.
3 Calculations on Babbage's machine were made from _____
_____
4 The Latin word _____ means 'finger, toe'.
5 To calculate means _____
6 Automatically means _____
_____

Read **all** of each paragraph about Modern Computer Games. Write the word from the box, which best fits the meaning, in the spaces.

1 A microprocessor can be programmed to [1]_____ many games. One of the first computer games, [2]_____ 'Pong', was a simple bat and ball [3]_____. 'Scramble', 'Space Invaders' and 'Chess' have since become [4]_____ with many [5]_____.

1	amuse	play	delight
2	shouted	exclaimed	called
3	game	joke	fun
4	like	popular	pet
5	mankind	people	individual

2 Some microprocessors are programmed for [1]_____ games. 'Speak and Maths' and 'Speak and Spell' are two games for [2]_____ and [3]_____. General knowledge games [4]_____ questions and sometimes play music while you think out the [5]_____.

1	learning	singing	finger
2	geology	arithmetic	botany
3	charming	casting	spelling
4	beg	ask	requested
5	total	notes	answers

3 The aim of the game 'Swarm' is to [1]_____ enemy aircraft. To score high points you must [2]_____ the space-craft while they are actually [3]_____. Always try to [4]_____ down a yellow space-craft as soon as it appears. Purple spacecraft are difficult to hit [5]_____ they fly at awkward angles. It is [6]_____ to keep away from the corners of the [7]_____ because you can easily be [8]_____ there.

1	destroy	killed	die
2	punched	hit	kicking
3	ambush	assault	attacking
4	aim	shoot	firing
5	or	because	although
6	silly	proper	wise
7	screen	triangle	circle
8	snare	trapped	arrest

Using reference books

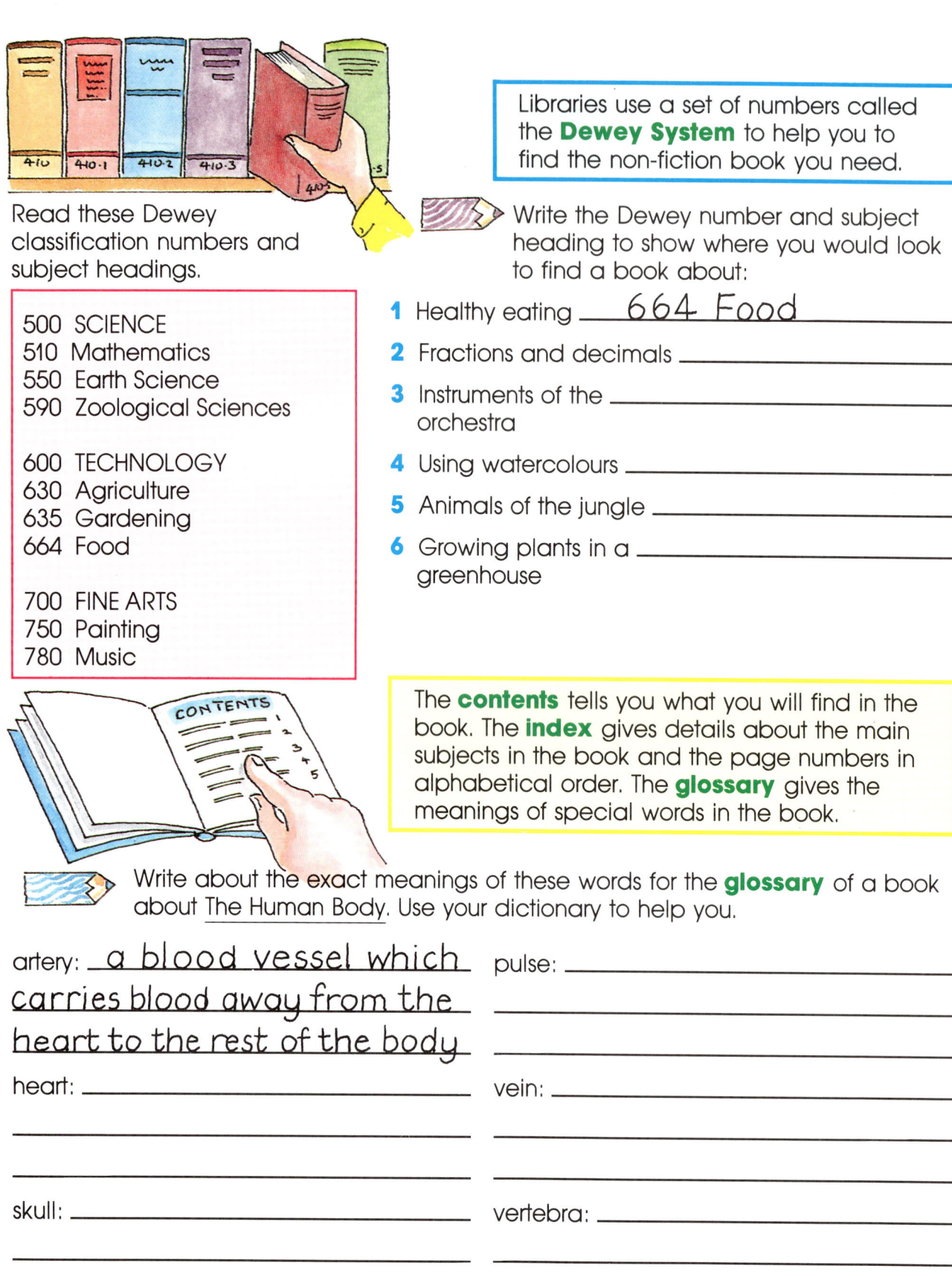

Read these Dewey classification numbers and subject headings.

500 SCIENCE
510 Mathematics
550 Earth Science
590 Zoological Sciences

600 TECHNOLOGY
630 Agriculture
635 Gardening
664 Food

700 FINE ARTS
750 Painting
780 Music

Libraries use a set of numbers called the **Dewey System** to help you to find the non-fiction book you need.

Write the Dewey number and subject heading to show where you would look to find a book about:

1 Healthy eating _664 Food_
2 Fractions and decimals _____
3 Instruments of the _____ orchestra
4 Using watercolours _____
5 Animals of the jungle _____
6 Growing plants in a _____ greenhouse

The **contents** tells you what you will find in the book. The **index** gives details about the main subjects in the book and the page numbers in alphabetical order. The **glossary** gives the meanings of special words in the book.

Write about the exact meanings of these words for the **glossary** of a book about The Human Body. Use your dictionary to help you.

artery: _a blood vessel which carries blood away from the heart to the rest of the body_

heart: _____

skull: _____

pulse: _____

vein: _____

vertebra: _____

Making notes

Read each sentence.

Cross out the words **not** important to the meaning.

Write the **key words** in each sentence as **notes**.

1 Your hair grows about 12mm (½ inch) each four weeks.

2 A grown-up's body contains about 5 litres (over 8 pints) of blood.

3 A grown-up's lungs hold 3 litres (5 pints) of air.

4 You use 200 different muscles every time you walk.

1 _____

2 _____

3 _____

4 _____

Read each paragraph.

Write **notes** for each paragraph.

1 A bruise is a blue-black mark on the skin. A freckle is a light brown spot on the skin. A verruca is a small, hard growth on the skin.

2 Your incisor teeth are for cutting and chopping food. Pointed, canine teeth are for tearing food. Molars, at the back of your mouth, are for grinding food.

3 Your eye has three main layers. The outer layer is the white of the eye. The coloured middle part is the iris. In the centre of the iris is a black opening called the pupil.

1 _____

2 _____

3 _____

Test your progress

✏️ Write each set of nouns in **alphabetical order**.

Victoria _____   Italy _____   mole _____

Elizabeth _____   Iceland _____   mosquito _____

James _____   Israel _____   moa _____

Henry _____   Ireland _____   mouse _____

George _____   India _____   moose _____

✏️ Draw lines to link the **antonyms**.   ✏️ Draw lines to link the **synonyms**.

like	depart		edge	observer
common	minimum		inside	margin
inferior	dislike		build	interior
maximum	uncommon		spectator	falter
arrive	superior		hesitate	construct

✏️ Put the correct **punctuation mark** in each balloon.

1 The children 🎈 s mother opened the door 🎈

2 🎈 Can Rangi and Anwar come to tea tomorrow 🎈 asked Jan 🎈 because I 🎈 m having a party 🎈

3 🎈 They 🎈 d be delighted 🎈 🎈 exclaimed Mrs. Singh 🎈

✏️ Complete these words with the correct **spelling**.

1 `t|h| | |f| ` a person who steals

2 `r|e|c| | |v|e` to accept something which is given

3 `p|r|e|c| | | | ` very valuable

4 `d| | | | | |t|e|r` someone's female child

5 `b|e|g| | | | |i|n|g` a starting point

6 `W|e| | | | |d|a|y` the fourth day of the week

7 `F|e|b| | | | |y` the second month of the year

8 `c| | | | |e` a round, flat shape

9 `d|i|s| | | | |r` to go out of sight

10 `C| | | | | | |s` December 25th

✏️ Colour in your correct result on the ladder and your mistakes on the snake.

30

 Draw a ring round the **subject** and underline the **verb** in each sentence.

1 The President arrived at the airport.
2 He waved to all the waiting crowd.
3 An important official greeted the visitor.
4 A brass band played the National Anthem.
5 Everyone cheered loudly.

 Write **past**, **present** or **future** to show the **tense** of the verb in each sentence.

1 I am happy today. _____
2 I saw a rainbow. _____
3 Yesterday I ate an apple. _____
4 Father is at home. _____
5 I will see you tomorrow. _____
6 Jack ran away. _____
7 Bach composed music. _____
8 Can you see the bird? _____

 Draw lines under the **verbs** and rings around the **adverbs**.

1 We waited hopefully.
2 The boy answered instantly.
3 The cat ran away.
4 I often play the piano.
5 Do crabs walk sideways?
6 She frequently comes to tea.

 Draw lines under the **nouns** and rings round the **adjectives**.

1 exotic, yellow roses
2 the secret, valuable jewel
3 a fine, Indian sari
4 poisonous, red berries

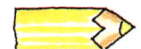 Underline the **pronouns** in these sentences.

1 Sandra lost her purse and John lost his ticket.
2 "Where have you been?" she asked.
3 Give me some money then we can all have ices.
4 The children decided that they would return to their school.

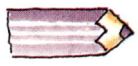 Colour in your correct result on the ladder and your mistakes on the snake.

31

Answers

Page 2

Bawden, Pearce, Ransome, Uttley, Williams
Adams, Aesop, Alcott, Anderson, Appiah
Beckett, Bell, Bennett, Berg
Betts
Gard, Garfield, Garland, Garner, Garvey
Oliver Twist

Page 3

1st part: cash, appal, blend, bluff
2nd part: lush, fawn, gulf, kebab
3rd part: phobia, mural, rouse, pride
4th part: septic, tamper, sole, vice
false false true false
true

Page 4

2 adjective **3** pronoun **4** verb
5 adjective **6** verb

1 Tom, he, his **2** children, they **3** Jane, John, We
4 mother, her, she

Page 5

old owls metal
2 old **3** terrible **4** burning
5 long **6** hunched
7 bony **8** rusty

Page 6

1 ✓ 4 ✓

1 One of my hobbies is cooking. For a Victoria sponge I use self-raising flour, soft margarine, caster sugar and eggs. Although butter has an excellent flavour you can make a very good cake with margarine. Eggs should be at room temperature and not used straight from the refrigerator.
2 Land's End is the southwest tip of the British mainland. Each year over a million people visit the area. Just over a mile offshore is the Longships reef. This danger to ships is guarded by the Longships lighthouse.

Page 7

2 A policeman (ran after him).
3 The angry shopkeeper (waved his fist).
4 A crowd (gathered near the scene).
1 Two silly sheep (wandered away from the flock).
2 The old shepherd (gave a short whistle).
3 His sheep dog (crept quietly round the wanderers).

4 The flock (was soon together again).
2 Some children, have **3** We, were **4** They, go **5** I, meet
6 James, does

Page 8

pitiful, pathetic beg, plead
crowd, multitude lively, active
locality, district inactive, idle
ridiculous try outside
mimic edge make yield
small clear

Page 9

ghastly hideous delicious
soiled beautiful aged
wealthy feeble fragrant

Page 10

1 You find geographical information in an atlas.
2 They learn about the Earth's surfaces etc.
3 'Atlas' comes from the name of a Greek giant.

Page 11

2 continent, large, mass, land
3 Asia, world's, largest, continent
4 Greenland, largest, island, world
5 longest, river, world, Nile
1 lake, area, water, surrounded, land
2 tributary, river, flows, another, river
3 river, stream, water, flowing, another, river, sea, lake
4 ford, shallow, place, people, wade, drive, across, river

Page 12

aught: taught, daughter, slaughter
ought: ought, bought, thought, brought
ance: entrance, performance, balance, substance
ious: suspicious, precious, delicious, previous

1 caught, slaughter
2 suspicious, previous
3 entrance, performance
4 thought, ought

pig crab trout
eel crow

Page 13

2 what is **3** are not **4** he is
5 has not **6** could not
1 I've **2** where's **3** isn't
4 she's **5** can't **6** wouldn't
2 sailor's **3** Mother's **4** horse's
5 Paul's **6** Spot's
1 birds' **2** girls' **3** dogs'
4 ladies' **5** knives'

Page 14

1 main **2** auxiliary **3** auxiliary
4 main **5** main **6** auxiliary
1 are **2** were **3** was **4** is **5** is
6 were
1 have **2** being **3** has **4** been
5 am **6** be
auxiliary supporting
additional supportively

Page 15

2 past **3** future **4** past
5 future **6** present
2 carved **3** designed **4** invented **5** composed **6** discovered
2 fought **3** came **4** saw **5** flew
6 brought

Page 16

detect, conceal fresh, rancid
ascend, descend
2 begin **3** contract **4** minimum
5 attentive
impossible disobedient
unsuitable unhealthy
illegible disapprove
1 Unsuitable, unhealthy
2 impossible, illegible
3 disapprove, disobedient

Page 17

dangerous breakable blissful
colourful/less
1 harmful **2** remarkable
3 hopeless **4** courageous

Page 18

c) The Origin of the Olympic Games
b) Athletic Events on the Second Day of the Festival
1 The Olympic Games originated at Olympia in Greece.
2 They were timed to take place between harvesting grain and gathering grapes and olives.
3 The Pentathlon consisted of five events etc.

Page 19

1 1 command **2** still **3** pistol
4 first **5** or
2 1 teams **2** also **3** injury
4 between **5** net
3 1 competitions **2** her
3 or **4** together **5** are

Page 20

Subject	Predicate
2 Dentists	extract teeth.
3 Soldiers	protect their country.
4 A judge	presides in court.
5 An optician	tests eyesight.

1 or **2** but **3** and